IMAGES OF WAR

THE M12 GUN
MOTOR CARRIAGE

Dedication

To the men of the 557th and 558th Field Artillery Battalions, who
led the way for heavy self-propelled artillery.

IMAGES OF WAR

THE M12 GUN MOTOR CARRIAGE

RARE PHOTOGRAPHS FROM WARTIME ARCHIVES

DAVID DOYLE

Pen & Sword
MILITARY

AN IMPRINT OF PEN & SWORD BOOKS LTD.
YORKSHIRE - PHILADELPHIA

First published in Great Britain in 2018 by
Pen & Sword Military
An imprint of
Pen & Sword Books Ltd
Yorkshire – Philadelphia

ISBN 978 1 52674 352 7

A CIP catalogue record for this book is
available from the British Library.

Typeset in 12/14.5 Gill Sans by
Aura Technology and Software Services, India
Printed and bound in India by Replika Press Pvt. Ltd.

Pen & Sword Books Limited incorporates the imprints of Atlas, Archaeology, Aviation, Discovery, Family History, Fiction, History, Maritime, Military, Military Classics, Politics, Select, Transport, True Crime, Air World, Frontline Publishing, Leo Cooper, Remember When, Seaforth Publishing, The Praetorian Press, Wharncliffe Local History, Wharncliffe Transport, Wharncliffe True Crime and White Owl.

For a complete list of Pen & Sword titles please contact

PEN & SWORD BOOKS LIMITED
47 Church Street, Barnsley, South Yorkshire, S70 2AS, England
E-mail: enquiries@pen-and-sword.co.uk
Website: www.pen-and-sword.co.uk

or
PEN AND SWORD BOOKS
1950 Lawrence Rd, Havertown, PA 19083, USA
E-mail: Uspen-and-sword@casematepublishers.com
Website: www.penandswordbooks.com

Contents

Acknowledgements

A number of people and institutions were involved in creating this book. Among these are Tom Kailbourn, Jim Gilmore, Scott Taylor, Joe DeMarco and Gordon Blaker at the US Army Field Artillery Museum, the staff of the National Archives, as well as the Patton Museum, US Army Ordnance Museum and

Although only 100 examples were produced, the 155mm Gun Motor Carriage M12 served with distinction as an infantry support weapon and in particular as a bunker-buster during the US assault on the Siegfried Line in the winter of 1944–45. Here, an M12 nicknamed 'Aiming Circle Annie' assigned to the 558th Field Artillery Battalion fires on enemy targets along the Moselle River in France on 8 September 1944. (*National Archives*)

US Army Transportation Museum. Providing previously unpublished photos of the M12 in use were Dan Ballou, who provided photos taken by his father, as well as Bill Larkin, who allowed the use of images furnished to his website devoted to the 558th Field Artillery Battalion. No one is more appreciated in this endeavor more than my wife Denise, whose tireless scanning of photos and copying of documents assembled the material from which this is drawn, at the same time most likely making her more knowledgeable about military equipment than she ever really wished to be!

Introduction

The ability to rapidly ready heavy artillery for firing – as well as rapidly withdraw the field pieces from the firing position – has what one would think is an obvious advantage on the battlefield. Despite this, the development and deployment of the M12 155mm gun initially met with some opposition.

Nevertheless, beginning in 1941, work started on developing a 155mm self-propelled gun based on the M3 Medium Tank chassis. The trial vehicle, built by Rock Island Arsenal, was designated T6. To accommodate the large, rear-mounted weapon – a French-made M1917 155mm gun – the engine was relocated forward to a position just behind the driving compartment. A hydraulically-operated spade was mounted at the rear of the vehicle, which was lowered during firing to anchor the vehicle against the recoil. When retracted into the travelling position it provided a seat for two of the six crewmen.

After testing and modification, the M12 was placed into production by the Pressed Steel Car Company. All these vehicles had the three-piece differential housing, but

Developed in 1938, the M1 was the US Army's most advanced 155mm gun prior to the nation's involvement in the Second World War. The gun was mounted on the M1 carriage with integral two-axle suspension, the trails being supported by a separate limber while being transported.

It was the separate limber that was indicative of the shortcoming of this weapon. As seen here, the weapon had to be towed by a separate prime mover – in this case the M4 high-speed prime mover – but more commonly the Mack NO 7.5-ton truck. Preparing the gun for firing required disconnecting the prime mover, unlimbering the gun, spreading the trails and emplacing the weapon, all of which was time-consuming. (*National Archives*)

it was tilted slightly forward to align it with the relocated engine. The production vehicles lacked the hydraulically-operated rear spade, utilizing instead a hand-operated winch to raise and lower the blade. The co-driver's position was also considerably different from that of the pilot T6.

The production run was between September 1942 and March 1943, with a total of 100 units being built. Though a few were used by training units, most were placed in storage until February 1944 when the first of seventy-four of them were shipped to Baldwin Locomotive Works to be improved based on further tests and usage in training. This work continued until May 1944.

Three slightly different First World War surplus weapons were mounted, depending upon availability: the M1917, the M1917A1 and the M1918M1. The M1917 was French-built, the M1918 M1 was US-built; the M1917A1 had the French gun tube and the US breech.

Produced in conjunction was the M30 ammunition carrier. Initially trialed as the T14, the M30 shared the chassis of the M12 and was used to supply ammunition to the big guns. These vehicles were also built by Pressed Steel and, like the M12, were also modified by Baldwin. A total of 100 of the M30 were produced.

The new vehicles were fielded by the 557th and 558th Field Artillery Battalions, where they quickly proved the merit of the concept, and paved the way for successive generations of heavy self-propelled artillery.

GENERAL DATA

MODEL	M12
WEIGHT (pounds)	59000
LENGTH (inches)	266.5
WIDTH (inches)	105.3
HEIGHT (inches)	113.5
STANDARD TRACK WIDTH (inches)	16 9/16
CREW	6
MAX SPEED (MPH)	24
FUEL CAPACITY (US Gallons)	200
RANGE (miles)	140
ELECTRICAL (volts)	24 negative ground
TRANSMISSION SPEEDS	5F 1R
TURNING RADIUS (FEET)	31
ARMAMENT: MAIN SECONDARY	155mm NONE

ENGINE DATA

ENGINE MAKE/MODEL	Continental R975-C1
NUMBER OF CYLINDERS	9 radial
CUBIC INCH DISPLACEMENT	973
HORSEPOWER	350 @ 2400
TORQUE (pound-feet)	840 @ 1700
GOVERNED SPEED (rpm)	2400

COMMUNICATION EQUIPMENT

The M12 carried an M113 flag set.

Chapter 1

The T6 Prototype

In June 1941 the US Army authorized the production of a pilot vehicle to be designated 155mm Gun Motor Carriage T6. Work on the pilot began the following month at the Rock Island Arsenal in Illinois. The vehicle mounted a 155mm Gun M1918M1 and its recoil mechanism and top and bottom carriages on a converted M3 medium tank chassis. It was completed in January 1942 and delivered to the Aberdeen Proving Ground for testing. (*Patton Museum*)

The T6 was assigned US Army registration number 307053. The 155mm gun lacked a gunner's shield. The barrel rests on a travel lock mounted on the front plate of the driver's compartment. A side escape door was on each side of that compartment. (*Patton Museum*)

The side of the left sponson of the T6 was taller to the rear to provide added protection to the two crewmen who were seated there. To the rear of the hull was the hydraulically-operated trail and spade, which transmitted recoil forces to the ground during firing. (*Patton Museum*)

A GI stands next to the T6 to provide a sense of scale. The driver and assistant driver each had a direct-vision door with a vision block. The armored cover of the final drive assembly is the three-piece type associated with M3 and very early M4 medium tanks. (*Patton Museum*)

The spade of the T6 is seen in the raised position from the rear. During tests at Aberdeen Proving Ground in March 1942, the hydraulic lifting cylinders of the trail and spade failed due to firing shock and it was necessary to redesign the lifting mechanism. (*Patton Museum*)

Above: The T6's running gear was the same as the M3 medium tank, with three bogie assemblies on each side, each with two wheels with size 20x9 rubber tires and a track return roller at the top of the bogie bracket. At the rear was a size 22x9 idler wheel. (*Patton Museum*)

Opposite above: The 155mm Gun M1918M1 was mounted in the rear of the T6, with the rear of the breech to the rear of the hull. A movable platform that slid back and forth on roller bearings was extended to the rear during firing for the crew to stand on. (*Patton Museum*)

Opposite below: The driver's compartment of the 155mm Gun Motor Carriage T6 had an overhead hatch on each side and a side door on each side. To the rear of the driver's compartment was the engine compartment containing a Continental R975-C1 nine-cylinder air-cooled radial engine; the roof and grilles of the engine compartment are visible from this angle. In the right and left sponsons were fuel tanks, with filler caps visible on top. The 155mm Gun M1918M1, its recoil mechanism, its top and bottom carriages, and the elevating hand wheel on the side of its top carriage are in view. (*Patton Museum*)

Above: To the left rear of the fighting compartment of the T6 was seating for two crew members. There was also seating for two crewmen on the raised spade and for two men in the driver's compartment. A good view is available of the recoil mechanism of the gun. (*Patton Museum*)

Opposite above: In a view of the T6 from the rear with the spade lowered, the gun and its recoil assembly are mounted on the upper carriage, with a deep U-shaped cut-out to allow for elevating the gun. The upper carriage rotated on the fixed bottom carriage, bolted to the floor. (*Patton Museum*)

Opposite below: The 155mm Gun M1918M1 on the T6 is at maximum elevation and maximum left traverse. The gun had a maximum elevation of 30 degrees, depression of 5 degrees and traverse of 14 degrees to the right and left of the longitudinal centerline of the vehicle. (*National Archives*)

Above: The operating mechanism of the spade included a hydraulic hoist on each outboard side, with two hydraulic tipping cylinders between the hoists. This mechanism proved trouble-prone during tests; for example, the hydraulic lines were repeatedly severed. (*Patton Museum*)

Opposite above: The bottom carriage was bolted to the floor of the T6 and provided a mount on which the upper carriage and gun traversed. On the inner face of the raised front of the unit was a traversing sector which engaged with the traversing gear of the top carriage. (*Patton Museum*)

Opposite below: The top carriage, as seen from the front, had a trunnion bearing on each side of the top, an elevating hand wheel on the left side and a traversing worm gear on the lower front. The traversing hand wheel is mostly hidden to the rear of the elevating hand wheel. (*Patton Museum*)

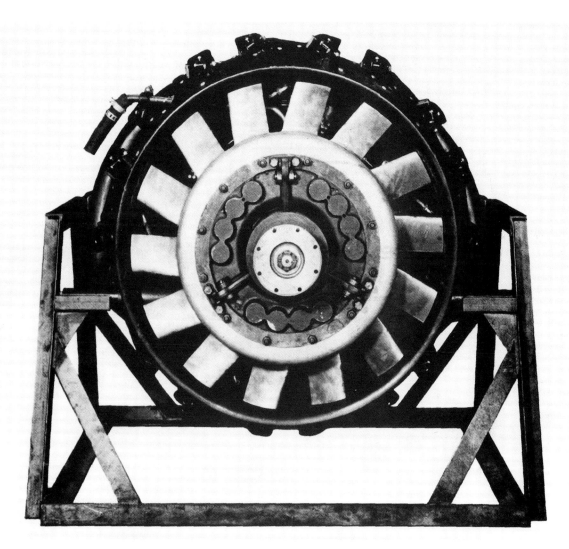

Above: For better air circulation for the air-cooled R975-C1 engine, a fan was mounted on the front. At the center of the engine are the clutch spindle and the companion flange. A very short propeller shaft was attached to the companion flange and to the transmission. (*Patton Museum*)

Opposite above: As seen from the rear of the top carriage, the nearer hand wheel is the traversing and the one to the front of it is the elevating. Inside the bottom of the carriage is the elevating worm gear, which engaged the elevating quadrant on the bottom of the recoil mechanism. (*Patton Museum*)

Opposite below: Powering the 155mm Gun Motor Carriage T6 was a Wright R975-C1 Whirlwind nine-cylinder radial engine, built under license by Continental Motors. Seen here from the rear, the engine is mounted on a support beam which is installed on a work stand. (*Patton Museum*)

Above: With its cover removed, the engine compartment of the T6 is viewed facing towards the front. At the bottom is the upper part of the engine support beam, above which is the exhaust manifold. In the left background is the top of the transmission oil cooler. (*Patton Museum*)

Opposite above: In a view of the left front corner of the engine compartment of the T6 with the engine removed, to the right of center is the transmission oil cooler and to the lower left are the clutch-release bearing and, to the front of it in the opening, the U-joint companion flange. (*Patton Museum*)

Opposite below: In the front right of the engine compartment is the engine oil cooler (left of center), to the right of which is the oil tank and breather. At the lower center is the lower engine-compartment shroud. The upper shroud was installed when the engine was in place. (*Patton Museum*)

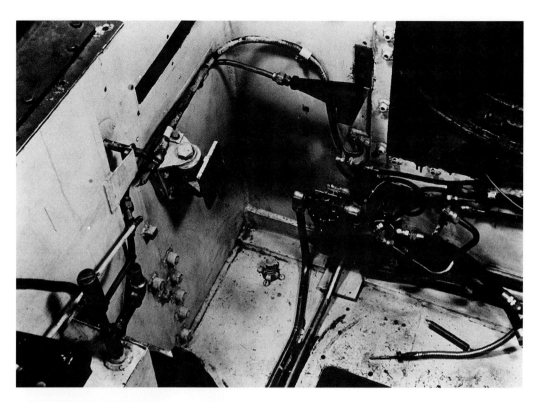

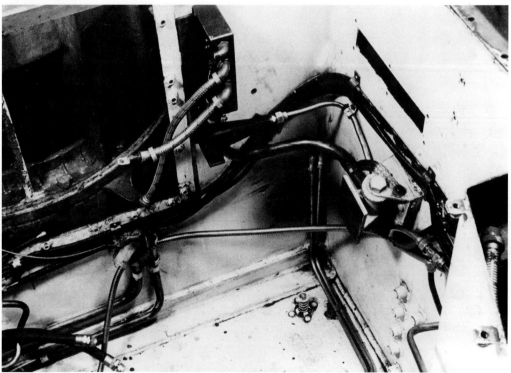

Above: In an 18 February 1942 photo taken at Aberdeen Proving Ground, with the spade lowered, a view is available of the two crew seats to the left, the firing platform, the top and bottom gun carriages and the rear of the 155mm gun's recoil mechanism. (*National Archives*)

Opposite above: In the right rear of the engine compartment with the engine removed, jutting from the side of the hull to the left of center is the right bracket for the engine support beam. At the upper center is one of four fire-extinguisher discharge nozzles in the compartment. (*Patton Museum*)

Opposite below: In a close-up view of the rear left corner of the engine compartment, the left bracket for the engine support beam is to the right. Visible through the opening to the left is the front of the bottom carriage of the 155mm gun, to the right of which is the rear terminal box. (*Patton Museum*)

Above: During evaluations of the T6 at Aberdeen Proving Ground on 18 February 1942, the gun is elevated, illustrating the interference of the loading platform with the gun breech during firing. The platform would be corrected for the production 155mm GMC M12s. (*National Archives*)

Opposite above: The spade of the 155mm GMC T6 is dug into the ground during tests at Aberdeen Proving Ground on 18 February 1942. The hydraulic cylinders that raised the spade would fail during testing the following month and would be replaced with improved ones. (*National Archives*)

Opposite below: The T6 is deployed in firing position during tests at Aberdeen, with the spade dug into the ground and the firing platform extended to the rear of the hull. An arrangement of blocks and slats of unknown purpose are attached to the front and the rear bogie brackets.

U.S.A 307053

The 155mm gun of the T6 is at maximum elevation and the spade is sunk well into the ground. During tests at Aberdeen in the late winter of 1942, it was determined that the spade worked satisfactorily in soft or wet ground, but not when the ground was frozen. (*Patton Museum*)

Chapter 2

The M12

The T6, above, was standardized as the 155mm Gun Motor Carriage M12. The Army ordered fifty M12s in July 1942 and another fifty in the following month. It was similar to the T6, with some revisions including a gunner's shield and winch-operated spade. (*National Archives*)

The same M12 shown in the preceding photo, US Army registration number 4055524, is observed from the rear. This was the thirty-fifth vehicle of the initial contract of fifty M12s. The spade was redesigned from that of the T6, with a smaller size and lighter weight. (*National Archives*)

M12 registration number 4055516 is undergoing tests at the Ordnance Operation, General Motors Proving Ground, on 8 November 1942. On the right side, the sponson had an uninterrupted side from the rear of the hull to the front of the driver's compartment. (*Joe DeMarco collection*)

In a view of M12 registration 4055516 from the left, the side of the left sponson ends at the rear of the driver's compartment door. The M12s had the later type of bogie brackets with the return roller offset to the rear and a steel skid on top of the bracket. (*Joe DeMarco collection*)

M12 registration 4055524 is parked at a test ground. The left side of the driver's compartment retained the door but the right side of the compartment lacked one, being filled in with an extension of the sponson. Atop the left sponson is a spare grouser box. (*Patton Museum*)

Above: The system of winch, cables and sheaves by which the hand winch raised and lowered the spade of the M12 is visible in this overhead photo. The winch and cables replaced the hydraulic lifts of the T6 spade, which had proved unsatisfactory in trials. To the rear of the winch is an ammunition loading tray with two handles on each side. The spade was redesigned from that of the T6, with four instead of three vertical partitions and eight prongs to facilitate the digging in of the spade. (*US Army Transportation Museum*)

Opposite above: On 23 September 1943 this M12 marked with the number 8313 was undergoing tests at the Ordnance Operation, General Motors Proving Ground. A thin sheet of steel, possibly representing a proposed shield, was on the right side of the 155mm gun mount. (*Patton Museum*)

Opposite below: An M12 is seen from above with the spade raised. Atop the right sponson are rammer-staff sections and, adjacent to the gun carriage, the hand-operated spade winch. On the left sponson are a grouser box and seats with cushions for two of the crewmen. (*Patton Museum*)

THE FIELD ARTILLERY BOARD
FORT BRAGG, N.C.

Neg. No.   29 – 1943   Date   3-3-1943
Exhibit   A – 1   File No. 451.2/x
Test No.   0-76-J   Item No. 396
155-mm Gun Motor Carriage M12.
ght rear view.

THE FIELD ARTILLERY BOARD
FORT BRAGG, N.C.

Neg. No.   29 – 1943   Date   3-3-1943
Exhibit   A – 2   File No. 451.2/x
Test No.   0-76-J   Item No. 396
155-mm Gun Motor Carriage M-12.
Left rear view.

Above: M12 registration number 4055514 is fitted with two bows to support a tarpaulin over the rear of the vehicle. An extra strip of armor plate has been welded atop the raised side of the hull where two crewmen were seated. This modification was found on some M12s. (*US Army Transportation Museum*)

Opposite above: An M12 is undergoing tests by the Field Artillery Board at Fort Bragg, North Carolina on 3 March 1943. A galvanized bucket is in its specified stowage spot on the spade seat. Two propellant charges in their packing tubes are stowed on the floor under the breech. (*National Archives*)

Opposite below: The same M12 in the preceding view is observed from the left rear. The right rear fender was severely dented. The M12 spade could be quickly lowered preparatory to firing by releasing the hand-winch ratchet and using the winch brake to ease the spade down. (*National Archives*)

The same M12 in the preceding photo has a tarpaulin over the two bows and a rear extension covering the 155mm gun breech and the spade. The vehicle is equipped with side skirts, although these often were not mounted on operational M12s. (*US Army Transportation Museum*)

Opposite: The spade is lowered on this 155mm Gun Motor Carriage M12 viewed from the upper rear during field trials in March 1943. The upper part of the spade as viewed from this angle included a stepped design that served as seating for two crewmen. (*National Archives*)

Above: The gunner is at the sight while the crewman to the left prepares to pull the lanyard to fire the 155mm gun on M12 registration number 4055524. The lanyard was a short cord that was hooked to the percussion-hammer operating shaft below the breechblock. (*National Archives*)

Opposite above: An M12 bulls its way through thick brush while advancing to a firing position; something that would be hard to accomplish for a towed artillery piece. During tests, the M12 proved its ability to be positioned for firing four times faster than a towed 155mm gun. (*National Archives*)

Opposite below: M12 registration number 4081010 was the seventh vehicle of the second contract of fifty M12s ordered by the US Army. An ammunition loading tray, tow cable and spade winch are atop the sponson. The small cylinder at the top of the breech was a counterbalance. (*Patton Museum*)

Above: A 155mm Gun Motor Carriage M12 has been loaded on a Landing Craft Tank (LCT) in an experiment at Aberdeen Proving Ground in late January 1944 to provide a landing craft with its own onboard fire support. The vehicle and gun were in traveling position. (*Joe DeMarco collection*)

Opposite above: The same M12 seen in the preceding photo is now configured in the firing position, with the spade lowered and the travel lock of the 155mm gun disengaged. Metal rims on the diamond-tread plates of the spade and trail served as retainers for two seat cushions. (*Joe DeMarco collection*)

Opposite below: A very grimy and heavily used 155mm Gun Motor Carriage M12 manufactured by the Pressed Steel Car Company is viewed from overhead in a photo dated 23 September 1944. A white recognition star is painted on top of the 155mm gun barrel. (*National Archives*)

Chapter 3

The T14

Designed to work together with the 155mm Gun Motor Carriage M12, left, was the Cargo Carrier T14. Based on the Medium Tank M3 chassis, the T14 carried ammunition and supplies for the M12 and also mounted a .50-caliber machine gun for defensive use. (*National Archives*)

A total of 100 examples of the Cargo Carrier T14 were produced by the Pressed Steel Car Company between October 1942 and March 1943. They were designed to transport forty 155mm shells and forty 155mm propellant charges as well as the corresponding fuses and primers. (*National Archives*)

ORD.
19523

Similar to the M12, the T14 had the engine directly to the rear of the driver's compartment. A fuel tank was in each sponson to the rear of the driver's compartment. The ammunition and propellant racks were located to the front of the ring mount. (*National Archives*)

Opposite: A Cargo Carrier T14 is viewed from the upper rear. The vehicle had a large tailgate for accessing the cargo compartment and this is lowered, showing two seat-belts for passengers on the built-in seat. Spanning the rear of the compartment is a ring mount. (*National Archives*)

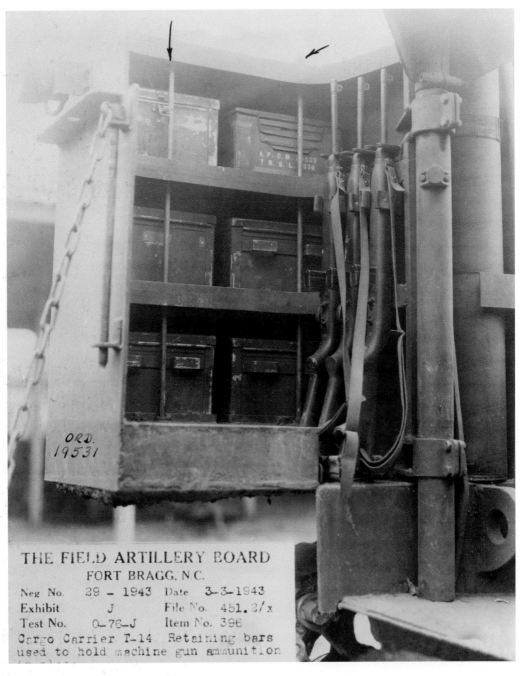

THE FIELD ARTILLERY BOARD
FORT BRAGG, N.C.
Neg No.   29 – 1943   Date   3–3–1943
Exhibit   J   File No. 451.2/x
Test No.   O–76–J   Item No. 396
Cargo Carrier T-14 Retaining bars
used to hold machine gun ammunition

During tests of a Cargo Carrier T14 by the Artillery Board at Fort Bragg, North Carolina in early 1943, this photograph was taken to document retainer rods that were inserted in the .50-caliber ammunition racks to keep the ammunition boxes in place. Space for ten 100-round .50-caliber ammunition boxes was provided. Adjacent to the ammunition racks is a rack holding three .30-caliber MI carbines; a fourth carbine was stored in the driver's compartment. (*National Archives*)

THE FIELD ARTILLERY BOARD
FORT BRAGG, N.C.
Neg. No.   29 – 1943   Date 3–3–1943
Exhibit   G   File No. 451.2/x
Test No.   0–76–J   Item No. 396
Cargo Carrier T–14. Broken Projectile rack.

During trials of a Cargo Carrier T14 conducted by the Field Artillery Board at Fort Bragg, North Carolina on 3 March 1943, the projectile rack was broken. The left side of the rack is viewed from the front, with the left air cleaner at the lower right. A crack that developed during tests is on the rack below the second hole down from the top right. (*National Archives*)

THE FIELD ARTILLERY BOARD
FORT BRAGG, N.C.

Neg. No. 29 – 1943   Date   3–3–1943
Exhibit   H   File No. 451.2/x
Test No. 0–76–J   Item No. 396
Cargo Carrier T–14. Broken hinges on
metal straps of upper rear compartment.

Broken retainer-strap buckles in the stowage compartment in the right rear corner of a Cargo Carrier T14 are documented in this photo taken during Field Artillery Board tests. These tests identified and recommended solutions to equipment failures such as this one. To the left is the right pedestal for the ring mount and to the right is a tailgate chain. (*National Archives*)

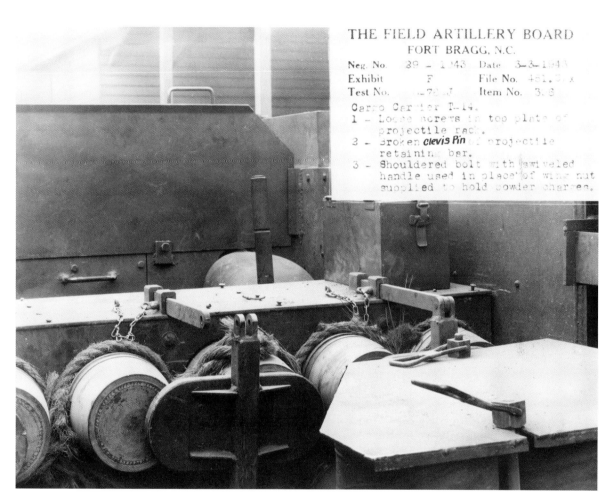

THE FIELD ARTILLERY BOARD
FORT BRAGG, N.C.
Neg. No. 39 - 1943 Date 3-3-1943
Exhibit F File No. 451.3 x
Test No. -72 J Item No. 3.6
Cargo Carrier T-14.
1 - Loose screws in top plate of
    projectile rack.
2 - Broken **clevis Pin** of projectile
    retaining bar.
3 - Shouldered bolt with swiveled
    handle used in place of wing nut
    supplied to hold powder charges.

Looking forward in the rear of a T14, the upper part of the projectile rack with shells loaded in it is observed. The bases of the shells face the viewer. In the lower left background is the top access panel at the rear of the engine compartment. (*National Archives*)

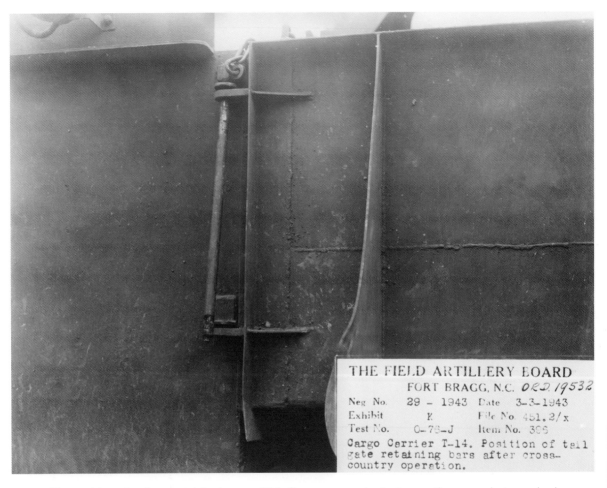

THE FIELD ARTILLERY BOARD
FORT BRAGG, N.C. *ORD. 19532*
Neg No.   29 - 1943   Date   3-3-1943
Exhibit   K   File No. 451.2/x
Test No.   0-78-J   Item No. 386
Cargo Carrier T-14. Position of tail
gate retaining bars after cross-
country operation.

The position of a tailgate retaining bar on a T14 after cross-country test operations was photographed for the Field Artillery Board at Fort Bragg in early March 1943. A retaining bar was on each side of the tailgate with a retainer chain attached to the top. (*National Archives*)

Cargo Carrier T14 US Army registration number 4080932 was photographed at the Aberdeen Proving Ground on 4 February 1943. The direct-vision doors of the driver's compartment are open and a foul-weather hood with windshield is on the driver's hatch. (*Patton Museum*)

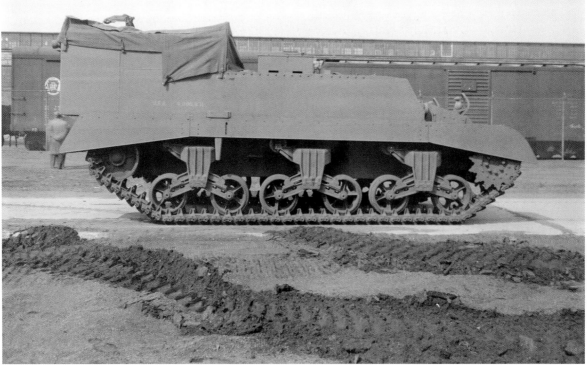

Above: This Cargo Carrier T14 was photographed at Aberdeen Proving Ground in February 1947. In addition to containing racks for 155mm ammunition, the T14/M30 carried tool boxes, spare parts, accessories and a large quantity of .50-caliber ammunition. (*US Army Ordnance Museum*)

Opposite above: In early 1944, hardly a year after the last of the T14s left the assembly lines, Baldwin Locomotive Works remanufactured 74 of the 100 T14s, which had been redesignated the Cargo Carrier M30 in September 1943. This vehicle appears to be unused. (*US Army Transportation Museum*)

Opposite below: The same T14 shown in the preceding photo, US Army registration number 4060971, is now sporting a tarpaulin cover over the rear compartment. The box with the two slots at the bottom to the front of the tarpaulin held thirteen track grousers; a similar box was on the opposite side. (*US Army Transportation Museum*)

Chapter 4

The M12 in Combat

'Adolf's Assassin', a 155mm Gun Motor Carriage M12 assigned to Battery A, 991st Field Artillery Battalion, conducts a fire mission near Kornelimünster in the Aachen district of Germany on 4 November 1944. The markings on this vehicle now have been applied to the sole surviving M12 at the US Army Field Artillery Museum, Fort Sill, Oklahoma. (*National Archives*)

In the autumn of 1944, ammunition stocks for US Army 155mm guns became depleted but, when it was determined that the guns could fire German 155mm shells, stocks of captured ammunition were pressed into service. This photograph, taken near Kornelimünster, Germany in November 1944, compares two 155mm shells: a US version (left) and a German version (right), to the rear of an M12 spade. (*National Archives*)

Above: The crew of an M12 prepares the 155mm gun for firing during field training at Camp Bowie, Texas in September 1943. The man in the foreground operates the rammer. The steps of the spade assembly provided a work platform for the crewmen serving the piece. (*National Archives*)

Opposite above: Crewmen crouch and brace themselves against the blast of the 155mm gun of an M12 during a live-fire training exercise at Camp Bowie, Texas, on 30 September 1943. Camp Bowie was one of the training sites for crews of 155mm GMC M12s. (*National Archives*)

Opposite below: Heavy camouflage netting is draped above and around the rear of an M12 Gun Motor Carriage nicknamed "Corregidor" as the 155mm gun fires against German forces near Saint-Lô, France, on 16 July 1944. "Corregidor" was assigned to the 991st Field Artillery Battalion. (*National Archives*)

Above: The 155mm Gun Motor Carriage M12, left, and the Cargo Carrier M30 were designed to operate together and the M12 could not operate long without support from the M30. These two crews of the 558th Field Artillery Battalion take a pause during training. (*Bill Larkin collection*)

Opposite above: Four 155mm Gun Motor Carriages M12 are deployed for firing during a field-training exercise in the United States. It was drills and practices such as this that enabled the crews to perform so effectively with relatively few M12s in the European Theater. (*Bill Larkin collection*)

Opposite below: Prior to embarking for the European Theater in July 1944, the 558th Field Artillery Battalion conducts a cross-country march during field training at the Hunter-Liggett Military Reservation, adjacent to Camp Roberts in Monterey County, California. (*Bill Larkin collection*)

Members of the 558th Field Artillery Battalion are in position for firing during training exercises. Communications personnel are in the foreground. In addition to the star insignia on the sponsons of the M12s, there is a star on top of both gun barrels. (*Bill Larkin collection*)

A crewman of an M12 is loading a propellant charge into the breech of the 155mm gun during a training exercise of the 558th Field Artillery Battalion. The man to the right holds a lanyard in his left hand, while to the left is the gunner. On the right fender is the letter 'A', signifying that this vehicle was assigned to A Battery. (*Bill Larkin collection*)

During the Stateside training period of the 558th Field Artillery Battalion, the 155mm gun of an M12 is in full recoil as it kicks up dust upon firing. Standing by the gun, mouth agape, is the gunner. The man to the left holding the lanyard is designated 'number 1'. (*Bill Larkin collection*)

Dust rises all around an M12 of C Battery, 558th Field Artillery Battalion at the instant of firing. The gunner has cupped his ears to protect them. To the left of the vehicle is number 1 and to the far left are loaders, designated numbers 2 and 3. (*Bill Larkin collection*)

Above: Interesting details abound in this photo of an M12 being prepared for firing. The crewman to the left carries aiming stakes. In the center foreground is a shell on a loading tray and more shells on a tarpaulin. A crewman is digging in the spade with a shovel. (*Patton Museum*)

Opposite above: Here again, the immediate environs of an M12 of the 558th Field Artillery Battalion have a puffy, dreamlike aspect as concussion from the gun stirs up the dust. Gun concussion was known to shatter the headlights of the M12 if they weren't removed before firing. (*Bill Larkin collection*)

Opposite below: In an image probably taken during training exercises in California, an M12 is emplaced and being prepared for firing. Under the front of the track is a collapsible chock, also called a wedge, which was placed there prior to firing to steady the vehicle. (*Bill Larkin collection*)

Above: In a thickly-wooded encampment, Arthur D. Ballou of the 557th Field Artillery Battalion sits on the barrel of the 155mm gun of 'Hari-Kari'. The tow cable is attached to the right tow clevis and is looped over the bow for quick access. A fabric dust cover is fitted over the muzzle of the gun. Ballou preserved this and the several following photos during his Second World War service. (*Dan Ballou collection*)

Opposite above: This moody and dramatic action shot was taken at the same site as the top photo on page 61. Battery B of the 991st Field Artillery Battalion reportedly fired the first US artillery shots to land on German soil when the unit shelled Bildchen on 10 September 1944. (*Patton Museum*)

Opposite below: Arthur D. Ballou is visible through the side door, sitting in the driver's seat of a 155mm Gun Motor Carriage M12 named 'Hari-Kari'. (*Dan Ballou collection*)

Above: Army personnel inspect a 155mm Gun Motor Carriage M12. The collapsible chocks are stored on the right fender. In the foreground is a Cargo Carrier M30 with markings for the 557th Field Artillery Battalion and another M30 is parked in the distance. (*Arthur Ballou via Dan Ballou*)

Opposite above: The crew of an M12 of the 557th Field Artillery Battalion poses with their vehicle. The man to the left holds one of the .30-caliber M1 carbines with which the crewmen were equipped. A large roll is stowed on top of the grouser box atop the sponson. (*Arthur Ballou via Dan Ballou*)

Opposite below: 'Betty' is painted on the barrel of the 155mm gun of this M12 of the 557th Field Artillery Battalion. The photo was taken from the left side of a Cargo Carrier M30, the left rear of which is visible in the foreground; note the star atop the sponson box. (*Arthur Ballou via Dan Ballou*)

An officer points to a stamped-spoke C85164 idler wheel on an M12 during an equipment inspection. The bogie wheels are probably the stamped-spoke C85163 type. The fender support above the head of the man to the right is severely bent. (*Arthur Ballou via Dan Ballou*)

Opposite: At a vehicle park in Salzwedel, Germany around the end of the Second World War, a wrecker crane is being employed to perform an engine change on a 155mm Gun Motor Carriage M12. The Continental R975-C1 engines were quite sensitive to abuse and drivers were carefully instructed in procedures to get the maximum possible life out of the engines, such as making sure to properly warm up the engine before moving the vehicle and always observing the recommended rpm and throttle and gear settings under various speed and terrain conditions. (*Arthur Ballou via Dan Ballou*)

Above: 'Dead Line' is marked above the registration number on this M12 of the 557th Field Artillery Battalion on a street in Germany. The left final drive unit reportedly has burned out and has been removed for replacement. An indistinct name is painted on the gun. (*Arthur Ballou via Dan Ballou*)

Opposite above: A Messerschmitt Bf 109 strafed this Cargo Carrier M30 with a full load of ammunition, igniting the ammo and causing a massive explosion that destroyed the vehicle. Two crewmen reportedly were killed and part of the vehicle was hurled across the road. (*Arthur Ballou via Dan Ballou*)

Opposite below: Several GIs inspect the destroyed Cargo Carrier M30. The left track was thrown completely off, and the rubber blocks on the right track burned so that only the track pins, bushings and connectors remained. Both the front fenders were also blown off. (*Arthur Ballou via Dan Ballou*)

Above: M12s of the 991st Field Artillery Battalion are emplaced on firing ramps to increase the guns' elevations while firing on Bildchen, Germany in September 1944. In the foreground, a crewman has removed a propellant charge from its fiber packing tube. (*Patton Museum*)

Opposite above: The same M30 as shown on page 69 is viewed from the left. The left side of the vehicle from the final drive unit (far left) to the rear was blown off in the blast. The engine lies in the wreckage to the rear of the driver's compartment. The top hatches were blown off their hinges. (*Arthur Ballou via Dan Ballou*)

Opposite below: Snow is falling around an M12 of Battery C, 557th Field Artillery Battalion near Morteau, France on 15 November 1944. Collapsible steel chocks, normally stored on the right front fender, have been deployed under the fronts of the tracks preparatory to firing. (*National Archives*)

Above: The gunner of an M12 named 'Buccaneer', US Army number 4081009, peers through the panoramic telescope in France on 25 November 1944. Sandbags are piled on the front of the vehicle for extra protection and the gun crew at the rear prepares to load a shell. (*National Archives*)

Opposite above Smoke is emanating from the breech of the 155mm gun on an M12 of the 981st Field Artillery Battalion, First US Army on 30 November 1944. The battalion was shelling German defenses in Kleinhau, Germany on the edge of the Hürtgen Forest. (*National Archives*)

Opposite below On 'Choo Choo Bam', M12 4081040 with the Third Army at Echternach, Luxembourg on 8 February 1945, a crewman holds a gunner's quadrant atop the breech, the gunner stands by the panoramic sight and a man wearing a tanker's helmet attaches the lanyard. (*National Archives*)

Above: A line of 155mm Gun Motor Carriages M12, including 'Alberta IV', US Army number 4081022 in the foreground, is lending fire support to the 11th Armored Division, laying down indirect fire on German targets near Büdesheim, Germany on 10 March 1945. (*National Archives*)

Opposite above: An M12 negotiates deep mud while advancing to provide fire support for elements of the 5th Infantry Division in assaults on the Siegfried Line near Berdorf, Luxembourg on 9 February 1945. In an attempt to gain traction, the entire crew has moved forward. (*National Archives*)

Opposite below: 'The Persuader', an M12 assigned to Battery B, 557th Armored Field Artillery Battalion, crosses a pontoon bridge in the vicinity of Linnich, Germany on 26 February 1945. Wooden pallets for stowing equipment off the ground are secured above the spade. (*National Archives*)

The barrel of the 155mm gun of an M12 is in full recoil as it dispatches a shell into a German pill-box near Seelbach, Germany on 18 March 1945. The vehicle was assigned to the 989th Field Artillery. Large but illegible writing is on the side of the hull. (*National Archives*)

A 155mm Gun Motor Carriage M12 advances to take on German pill-boxes near Niederschlettenbach, Germany on 20 March 1945. This vehicle has a unique stowage bin attached to the front of the right sponson, apparently fabricated from steel rods or bars. (*Patton Museum*)

Above: A Cargo Carrier M30 rolls through war-torn Weimar, Germany, around the time of the Nazi defeat in spring 1945. A machine gun is not mounted on the ring mount, a sign that hostilities had ended, at least in this sector. A tarpaulin is thrown over the ring mount. (*Arthur Ballou via Dan Ballou*)

Opposite above: A roadside track-replacement operation is under way on a Cargo Carrier M30 assigned to the 557th Field Artillery Battalion in Germany around the end of the Second World War. The replacement track is laid out on the road and the vehicle is being backed up to it. (*Arthur Ballou via Dan Ballou*)

Opposite below: The replacement track with extended track connectors on the outboard side has been installed on the M30 and a crewman is tightening a connector wedge. A symbol is present for the 5th Armored Division, to which the 557th became attached in late February 1945. (*Arthur Ballou via Dan Ballou*)

The 155mm Gun Motor Carriage M12, registration number 4055526, retained by Aberdeen Proving Ground and shown in this February 1947 view, displays the extended armor for the crew seats at the rear of the hull; the inboard edge of the front plate is angled. The boxes on the left fender held, front to rear, track blocks and track connectors. (*Patton Museum*)

Chapter 5

The M12 Preserved

The only known surviving 155mm Gun Motor Carriage M12 is this example, formerly on display at Aberdeen Proving Ground and now restored and displayed at the US Army Field Artillery Museum, Fort Sill, Oklahoma. It was repainted and, for display purposes, given markings to replicate 'Adolf's Assassin', an M12 assigned to Alpha Battery, 991st Field Artillery Battalion in North-Western Europe towards the end of the Second World War. As on the original 'Adolf's Assassin', the crest of the 991st Field Artillery Battalion is marked on the hull. (*US Army Field Artillery Museum*)

Above: The direct-vision doors for the driver and assistant driver are each held open by a single arm. Between the doors are the lowered travel lock and the ventilator hood. Both headlight assemblies are present, with a blackout marker lamp over the service headlight.

Opposite above: The M12s were mounted with three different 155mm guns: the M1917 of French manufacture and First World War vintage; the US-made M1918M1; and the M1917A1, an M1917 with the M21918A1 breech ring. The surviving M12 has an authentic M1917 gun. (*US Army Field Artillery Museum*)

Opposite below: Prior to restoration, the M12 was stored at Aberdeen in a state of deterioration, with a coating of rust on most of the steel surfaces and parts missing such as the right headlight assembly. Restoration entailed stripping the old paint and rust, treating the surfaces, and priming and painting.

Above: The three-piece final drive housing, bolted together at the flanges, is replete with casting marks. These marks included the foundry trademark, the part number and serial number, the type of steel and sometimes other information such as the date of manufacture.

Opposite above: Brush guards of bent and welded steel strips provided protection for the headlight assemblies. The cylinder on the side of the inboard brace holds a plug and retainer chain; when the headlight was removed, the plug was inserted in the socket to protect it.

Opposite below: The left headlight assembly and brush guard are viewed. In the background is the driver's direct-vision door in the open position, with the interior part of the vision block visible on the door. On the fender to the far right is a box for storing spare track blocks.

Above: In a view of the left side of the surviving M12, a side door is partly open on the driver's compartment. A similar door was not on the right side of the compartment as a stowage compartment was there. Two hatch doors are open atop the driver's compartment. On the front left fender is a track-block storage box, with a track-connector box to the rear of it. The armor around the two rear crew seats at the right rear of the hull has the extended upper plates found on some M12s. (*US Army Field Artillery Museum*)

Opposite above: Several types of double-pin tracks were used on M12s, including steel, with or without chevrons; rubber with chevrons; and plain rubber such as these. Usually, when a plain rubber-block track was employed, it was the T51, which was 16.56in wide.

Opposite below: Track connectors on each side of the tracks were secured to the track pins and also served as track guides. The sprocket is the type D47366, and it was fastened to the hub drum with thirteen hex-head screws. The hub is fastened to the final drive with eight studs and nuts.

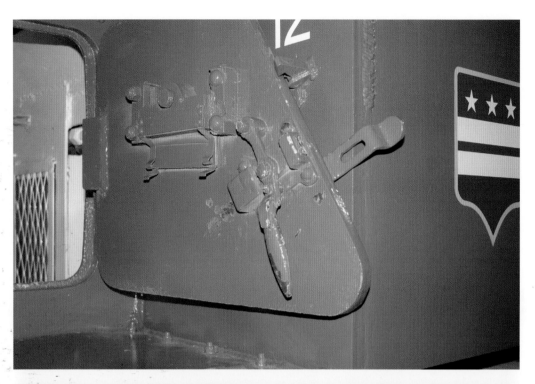

Above: The ceiling of the driver's compartment is seen through the driver's side door. The two top hatches are visible. Mounted to the ceiling is a dome light assembly. To the left is the welded joint between the ceiling and the frontal plate of the driver's compartment.

Opposite above: The interior of the driver's side door is observed close up, showing details of the locking handle and mechanism and the vision-block holder. A latch below the number 12 at the top held the door in place when open, preventing it from suddenly slamming shut.

Opposite below: In a view through the side door, on the rear bulkhead of the driver's compartment are ventilation grilles for the two oil coolers in the engine compartment. On the opposite side is a space where camouflage netting, technical manuals and other items were stored.

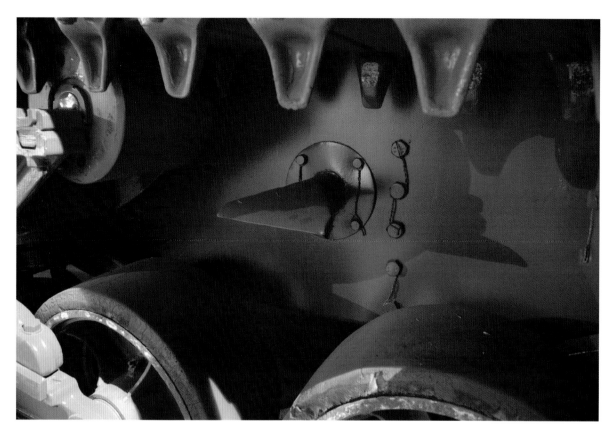

Above: Between the center and rear bogie assemblies on each side of the hull is an engine-exhaust tail pipe. Locking wires are wrapped around the hex screws that secure the tail-pipe flange to the hull and also around the hex screws adjacent to the tail pipe.

Opposite above: On each side of the M12 are three vertical volute bogie assemblies, each with two rubber-tired wheels on suspension arms that pivoted on a bogie bracket. On top of the bogie bracket was a skid and at the upper rear of the bracket was a return roller.

Opposite below: Welded to the side of the right sponson is a sheet-metal fixture that appears to be a holder of some sort. This feature dates back at least to recent decades when the vehicle was on display at Aberdeen Proving Ground and it most likely was installed while there.

Above: The left tail pipe is viewed from below, showing the fins inside the opening. Inside the hull between each tail pipe and the exhaust manifold was a flame arrester, on the floor of the fighting compartment to the rear of the rear engine-compartment bulkhead.

Opposite above: On each side of the M12 was a sponson brace, held at the top by a bracket welded to the sponson and attached at the bottom to a steel plate that was fastened with four hex screws to the front of the rear bogie bracket. The left brace is depicted here.

Opposite below: The left sponson brace is observed from another angle. Also in view are details of the rear bogie bracket at the lower left, including the casting seam running horizontally near the top of the unit. The screws on the brace plate are secured with locking wires.

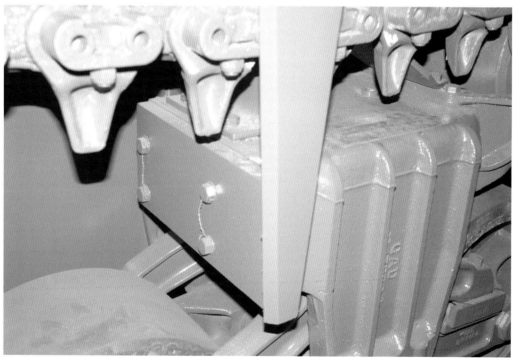

The bracket that secures the top of the sponson brace is seen close up. It is formed with two steel plates welded to the sponson to the front and the rear of the brace, to which an outer plate is welded. Details of the track connectors are also visible in this photo.

Opposite: The left sponson brace is viewed from the rear. A thick welded bead is present where the inner face of the bottom of the brace meets the steel plate screwed to the front of the bogie bracket. In view to the left is the center bogie assembly, with the rear wheel and rubber tire mounted on two suspension arms. Resting on the top of each suspension arm is a lever, through which forces of the flexing arms were transmitted to the two vertical volute springs. The wheels on this M12 are the five-spoke model D38501.

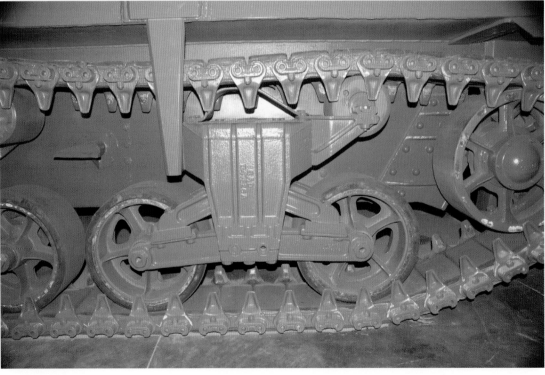

Above: At the rear of the suspension is the idler wheel. This was mounted on an eccentric spindle designed to permit adjustment of the wheel so as to adjust the track tension. To the front of the idler on the side of the hull is the front of the idler spindle bracket and its rivets.

Opposite above: All three of the bogie brackets on the left side of the M12 are in view here, as is the sponson bracket. The hex nuts on the bottoms of the track connectors were tightened onto threaded studs on wedges that served to hold the connectors to the track pins.

Opposite below: The left rear bogie assembly is observed from the side. The large casting to which the suspension arms are attached at the bottom is the bogie bracket. At the top of the bracket is a skid and projecting from the upper rear is a yoke supporting a track return roller.

The idler wheels on the surviving 155mm Gun Motor Carriage M12 are the D37916 version, with six open spokes, size 22-9. This type of idler wheel typically was used along with open-spoked bogie wheels. Casting marks are visible on the idler cap.

Opposite: In a view from the left rear of the M12, the three diamond-tread steps on the left fender are evident. The spade and trail assembly provided stepped, diamond-tread platforms for the loaders to stand on when the spade was sunk in the ground. Also in view are the 155mm gun breech, the top and bottom gun carriages, the traversing hand wheel and the rear of the gunner's shield. (*US Army Field Artillery Museum*)

Features of the M12 are observed from the left rear. Each curved rear fender is supported by a tubular brace from the rears of the sponsons and three steps are attached to the fender. The rear plate of the supplemental armor for the two crew seats at the left rear of the vehicle has an angled inboard edge and a small opening in it. The spade is held in the raised position by a chain and not by the support arms, the left one of which is visible on top of the spade trail. (*US Army Field Artillery Museum*)

Opposite: On the left rear of the M12 hull is one of the sheaves around which the cable for hoisting and lowering the spade assembly was routed. That cable dangles loosely here as it is not operable, but when it was operable and the spade was in the raised position, the cable generally was kept taut. Below the sheave is the bracket to which the spade support arm was pinned during travel.

This is the sheave at the upper left of the spade, part of the spade-hoisting mechanism. To the side of the sheave is the anchoring loop for the hoist cable. To the lower right is the left support arm of the spade, used for securing the spade in the raised position for travel.

Opposite: The front of the spade assembly is observed from the right side, showing the steel rims that served as retainers for the seat cushions. The top of the spade to the left of the photo served as the back for the two crew seats. The right support arm is missing; its bracket is in the foreground. Two seat-belt holders are between the seat rims and another one in damaged condition is next to the left support-arm bracket.

The entire left support arm is shown, including its hook end. The support arm pivoted on the bracket to the left. A matching arm was on the right trail. To the lower right is the lid of the stowage box that contained four .30-caliber MI carbines for the crewmen.

Opposite: In another view of the spade assembly from the right side, to the left is the diamond-tread plate to the bottom front of the crew seats. To the right is the lid for the weapon-stowage box. Two of its leaf-type hinges are visible. At the front center of the lid is the handle. In the foreground is the top of the right trail; the trails were the arms that supported the spade and pivoted on brackets at the rear of the hull.

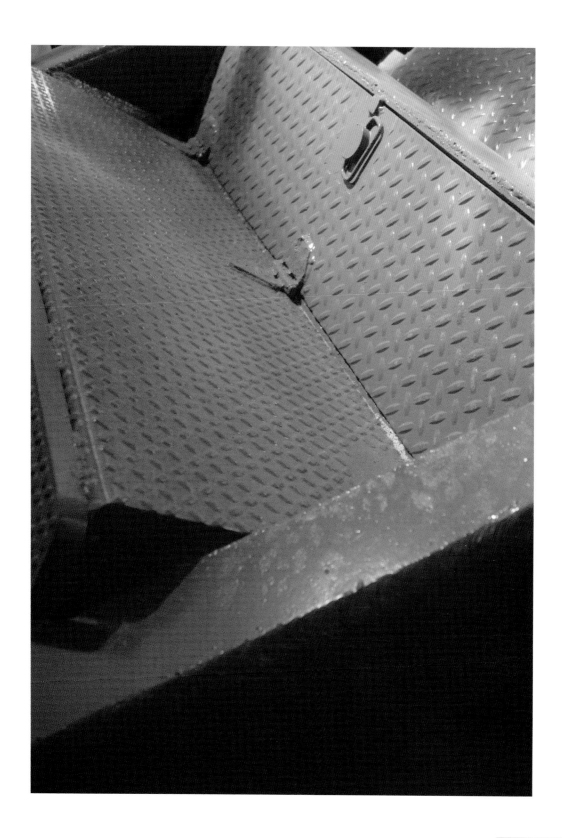

The front of the left trail pivoted on a bracket that was incorporated into the idler-spindle bracket. Visible below the cut-out in the diamond-tread plate is the large hex nut by which track tension was adjusted. Atop the front of the trail is welded a lifting eye.

Opposite: One of the floor plates is removed from the left rear of the fighting compartment, permitting a view down into the storage space. Tools and other equipment were stowed here. The missing plate had ring-shaped holders for three shells. A total of six shells were stored on the left side of the compartment and four on the right side. Curved cut-outs in the sill to the left were to provide clearance for the shells.

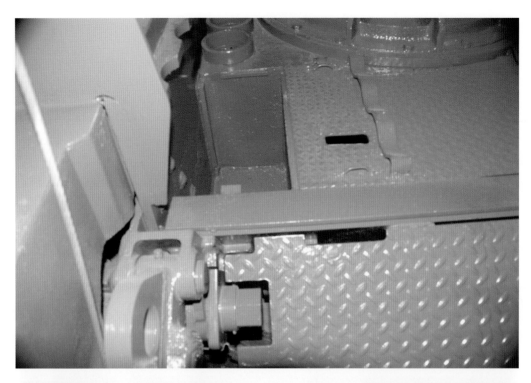

Above: The seating space for two crewmen at the left rear of the fighting compartment is shown. In service, seat cushions were present. Seat-belt holders are welded to the back plates. Below the seats are racks for propellant charges. To the right is the traversing wheel.

Opposite above: Facing forward from over the spade and trail assembly, at the bottom is the front of that assembly, to the front of which is the left rear of the crew compartment. At the top right is the base of the bottom carriage. To the left of it are several shell-holders.

Opposite below: Below the two crew seats (upper left) are racks for storing six 155mm propellant charges. Two more charges were stored in wells in the bottom carriage support and two were stored horizontally on retainer strips on the floor; the left strip is at the bottom center.

In each front corner of the fighting compartment is a heavy-duty oil-bath air cleaner for the engine. The left one is in the center background. The air cleaners took in air at the top intake and swirled it around inside, causing dirt in the air to settle on oil at the bottom of the filter. The air then passed through filter elements and clean air was sent to the carburetor. Another type of air cleaner observed on M12s was a large drum-shaped assembly.

The gunner had a rather cramped station between the sponson and the gun mount. The wheel facing the viewer was for traversing the piece, and to the front of it was the elevating hand wheel. Above the hand wheels are the mounts for the Panoramic Telescope M6 and the direct-sighting Telescope M53. The shield had a vision hole for the telescope and the top of the shield folded down when the panoramic telescope was used.

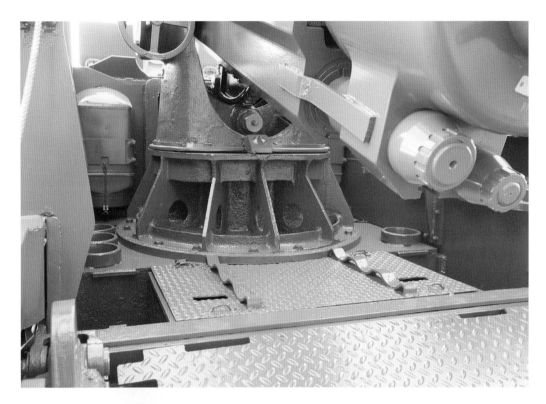

Above: To the rear of the bottom gun carriage is a removable floor plate with a hand-hold and retainer strips for stored 155mm propellant charges, the left one of which is in view. Footman loops were welded to the plate to receive hold-down straps for the charges.

Opposite above: A close view is offered of the top and bottom gun carriages from the rear. The upper carriage traversed on the fixed bottom carriage, which was bolted to the floor. To the upper right is the bottom of the 155mm gun breech, below which are, left to right, the recoil piston rod nut and the counter-recoil piston rod nut. The recoil and counter-recoil mechanisms are housed inside the cradle, which also served as a slide for the gun. Attached to the bottom of the cradle in the background is the elevation sector.

Opposite below: At the upper rear of the breech of the 155mm Gun M1917 is stamped 'PUTEAUX 1918', signifying that the Puteaux Arsenal in France produced the gun in 1918. Below is serial number 'USA No. 1190', below which is stamped 'No. 804'.

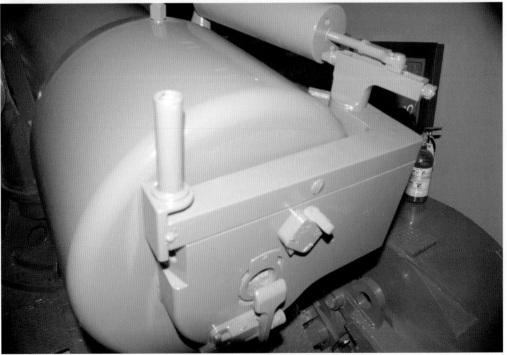

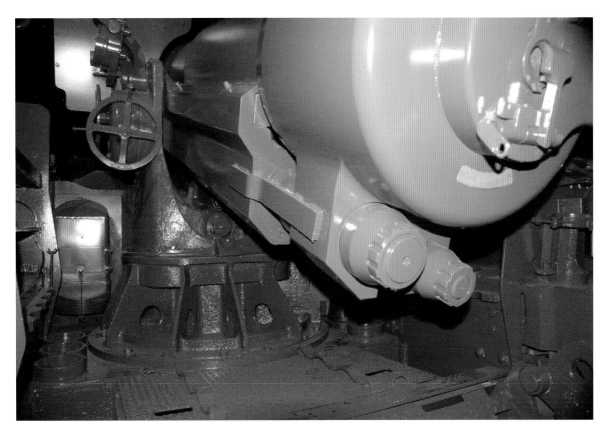

Above: The piston rods for the recoil, left, and counter-recoil, right, mechanisms protrude through the lug at the bottom of the breech. The nuts on the ends of these rods were present when the gun was to be fired and were removed when the gun was idle.

Opposite above: The geared elevation sector is at the center. The fitting to the rear of the sector bolted to the bottom of the cradle and the fitting with the round hole in it at the rear of the top carriage held a jack, which was removed when the gun was prepared for firing.

Opposite below: In a view of the 155mm gun breech, to the upper left is the operating handle for the breechblock. Towards the bottom of the breech is the percussion hammer and its operating shaft which, when pulled by a lanyard, ignited a primer, causing the piece to fire.

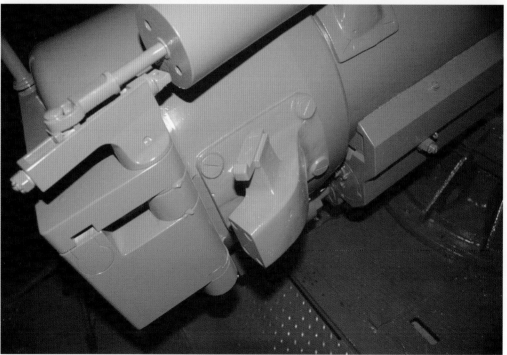

Above: The counterbalance, as viewed from the front, was a cylinder containing a spring and piston that exerted varying degrees of force through a tension rod on the breechblock to make it easier to open and close that heavy unit when the gun was elevated.

Opposite above: The gun's US Army serial number, 1190, is etched on a plate screwed to the breech below the breechblock carrier. 'No. 804' stamped on the breech below it appears to have been the original French serial number applied when the gun was manufactured.

Opposite below: On the right side of the breech are the breechblock carrier hinge-pin lugs. Projecting from the side of the breech to the front of these pins is the breechblock carrier stop, on top of which is the breechblock operating lever catch. At the top is the counterbalance.

Above: The surviving 155mm Gun Motor Carriage M12 is loaded on a transporter. A clear view is available of the spade, with its four partitions and the eight prongs on the lower edge. On the hull between the trails of the spade is the wrench for adjusting track tension. (*US Army Field Artillery Museum*)

Opposite above: The prongs are bolted to the bottom of the spade and even those relatively small parts had casting numbers on them: 41 is visible on one, and 264 is on two others. There was not a middle step on the right rear fender like the one on the left fender; instead, there was an indentation on the inboard side of the fender partway up. At the front of the fender is a bracket for a fire extinguisher. Above it is a double sheave for the spade-operating cable. To the right of the double sheave assembly is a latching bracket for the right support arm of the spade. (*US Army Field Artillery Museum*)

Opposite below: The right side of the hull is even along the top, lacking the raised area at the rear to protect two seated crewmen. The sponsons contained fuel tanks and stowage spaces. The object on the bottom of the barrel is a bronze clip for guiding the gun during recoil. (*US Army Field Artillery Museum*)

Above: The breechblock is not visible when the breech is closed. What is visible is the breechblock carrier, which held the interrupted-thread, revolving breechblock and housed the somewhat complex mechanism for locking and unlocking the breechblock. (*US Army Field Artillery Museum*)

Opposite above: Facing aft, at the bottom is the rear ventilation grille of the engine compartment. The manner in which the clips of the gun barrel fit in the slide of the cradle is apparent. To the left is the top of the right sponson; the hand-operated spade winch is not present.

Opposite below: On the far side of the front of the cradle is the front of the recoil cylinder. The recoil mechanism was variable, so the length of recoil varied according to the gun elevation. The disc with four holes is the air-relief valve at the front of the counter-recoil cylinder.

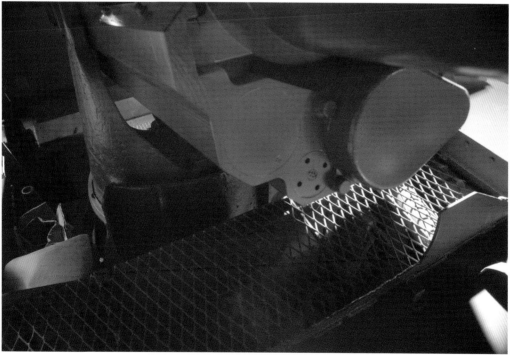

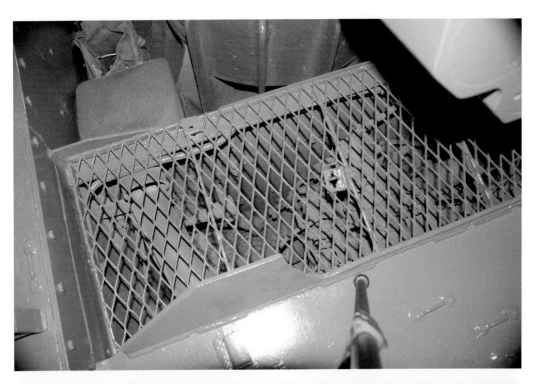

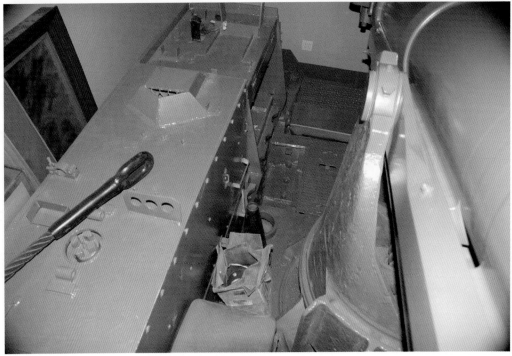

Above: Further back on top of the right sponson, in the foreground is a fuel-tank vent with an armored cover and a splash guard to the front, over which the loading tray was normally stowed. On top of the rear of the sponson are brackets for holding accessories.

Opposite above: The left side of the rear grille atop the engine compartment is viewed from next to the front of the gun cradle, upper right. Below the grille to the left is the right carburetor air intake, which has become detached from the top of the air cleaner to the upper left.

Opposite below: The top of the raised part of the right sponson coincided with the right fuel-tank cover. To the rear of the fuel filler in the foreground (its armored cover is missing) is a holder for three rammer-staff sections and mounting studs for the spade winch, not installed.

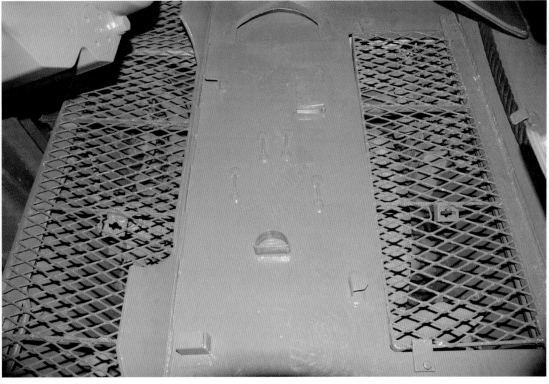

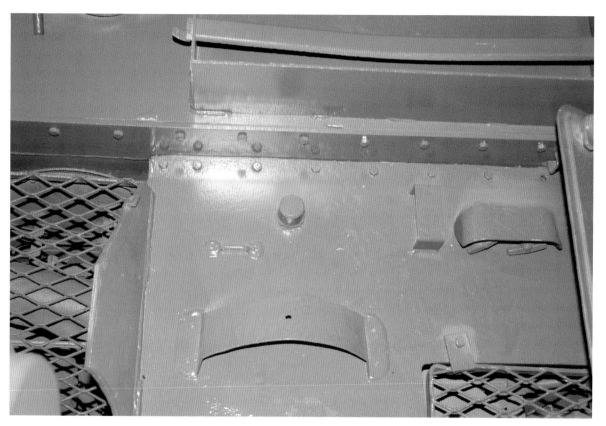

Above: Brackets for a shovel and a mattock head are on the left side of the engine-compartment cover. To the right is a small hood over the two pull handles for operating the fixed fire-extinguisher system. The two fire extinguishers were directly below this spot.

Opposite above: The top of the right sponson adjacent to the engine-compartment cover comprises the battery-compartment cover and has an inspection plate screwed to it next to brackets for the rammer-staff and aiming posts. A tow cable is present in its stowed position.

Opposite below: The engine-compartment cover is observed from the right side with the front of the gun cradle to the left. To the front of the rear grille is a splash guard with a recess in it to accommodate the gun in the travel position. Brackets for pioneer tools are on the cover.

Above: The left fuel-tank vent and tow-cable clamp are observed from a different angle. To the left is the lower part of the gunner's armored shield. A small storage case with a latch on top is mounted on the lower part of the shield.

Opposite above: To the front of the left sponson is the armored cover for the left fuel-tank filler, left, and the box for storing grousers. Two removable retainer slats are inserted in holes on the front and the rear of the box. To the far right is the driver's side door in the open position.

Opposite below: The fuel-tank cover of the left sponson has an armored vent towards the rear. Next to it is a clamp for the tow cable. To the lower left is the front left corner of the fighting compartment and the top of the left air filter. To the top left are crew seats and armor.

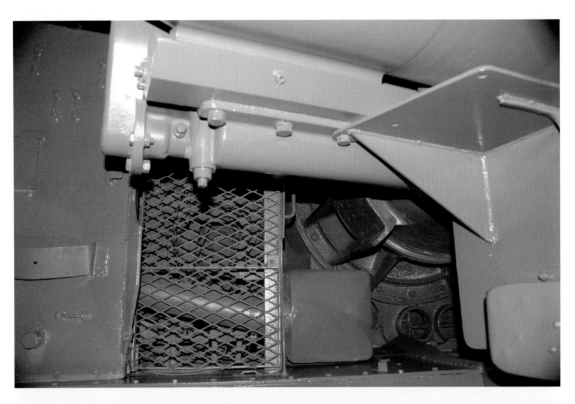

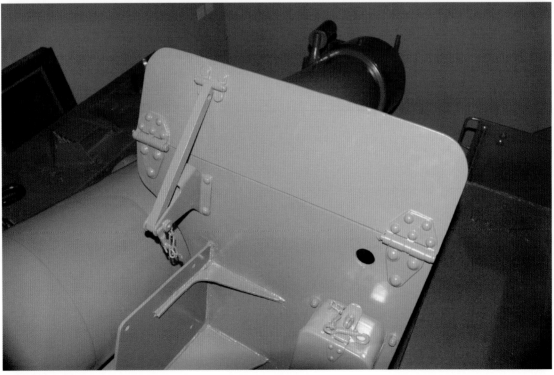

Above: Attached to the left trunnion of the gun mount are the mounts for the telescopes. The tall one to the right is the sight quadrant M1918A1, which held the M6 panoramic telescope. The one to the left is the telescope mount M40 for the M53 telescopic sight.

Opposite above: In a view from the left sponson looking down at the left air-cleaner (lower center) and the gun carriage, the bottom of the gun shield is to the right. The vertical plate with gusset jutting from the lower right of the shield is bolted to the side of the gun cradle.

Opposite below: The hinged top plate of the gun shield was lowered when the M6 panoramic telescope was used. The brace held the plate in the raised position. The round hole in the shield was the sighting aperture for the M53 telescopic sight. The breech is in the background.

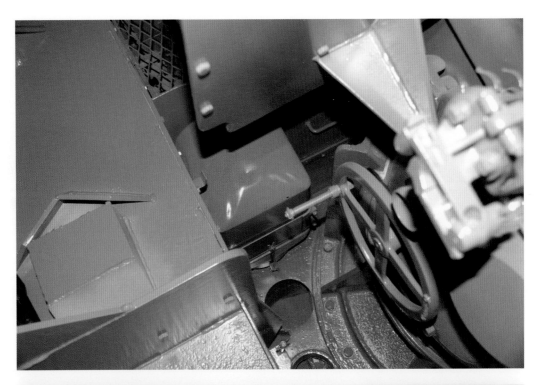

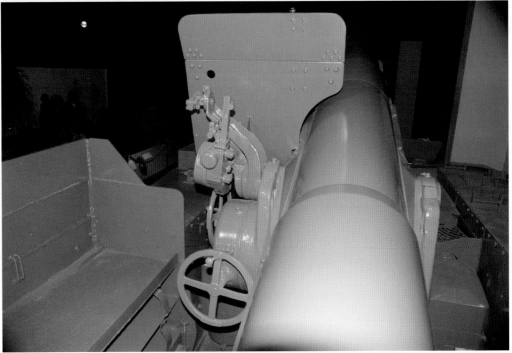

Above: Viewed from above the gun, the mount nearest to the trunnion is for the M53 telescope, used for direct fire at close and/or fast-moving targets. The further mount is for the M6 panoramic telescope, used for indirect-fire missions, generally against distant targets.

Opposite above: Below the gun-sight mounts is the elevating hand wheel, which is missing its grip. At the center is the left oil-bath air filter. To the left are the armored hood and the splash guard for the vent for the left fuel tank. At the top are the gun shield and the rear grille.

Opposite below: The elevating and traversing hand wheels are mounted on a gearbox on the side of the top carriage. Shafts from the gearbox transmitted power to the elevating and traversing worm gears within the top carriage. Above the gearbox are the two mounts for the sights.

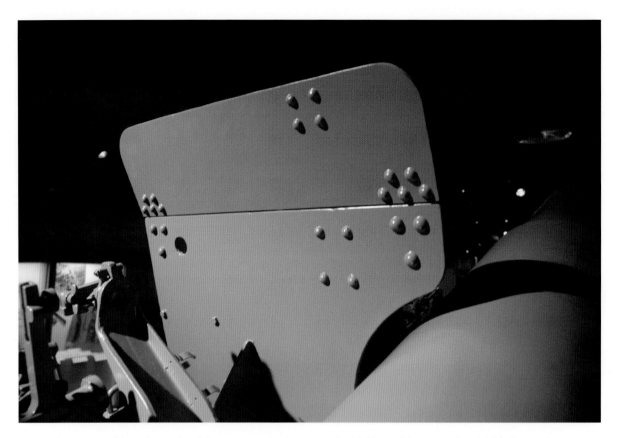

It was possible to keep the sight aperture in the gunner's shield small because the shield elevated or depressed in unison with the M53 telescope. A 14in extension was available for the M6 panoramic telescope so the top of the shield could remain raised.

Opposite: The fronts of the top and the bottom carriages of the 155mm gun mount are to the right, observed from the left side of the crew compartment. The bottom carriage has a beveled rim at the top that projects to the rear. The bottom surface of this rim is in contact with a projection on the front of the top carriage referred to as the traversing guide lug. To the left is the front bulkhead of the crew compartment, with removable panels with grab handles for accessing the engine compartment.

Above: The front grille of the engine compartment cover and the open hatches of the driver's compartment are viewed. Directly below the grille is the front of the engine. Latches and operating handles are on the interiors of the hatch doors. The tow cable is also in view.

Opposite above: The driver's direct-vision door is in the open position, viewed from above, to the left. To the right is the travel lock. After firing, the lock was raised and the gun barrel was lowered onto it and clamped. The process was reversed when the gun was to be fired.

Opposite below: The large box at the front of the left fender held six spare track links. The smaller box to the rear of it contained twelve spare track connectors and wedges, associated safety nuts and spare pins for the tow shackles. The rear of the left headlight assembly is in view.

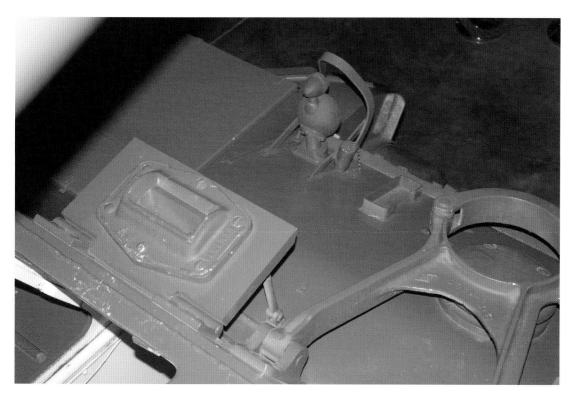

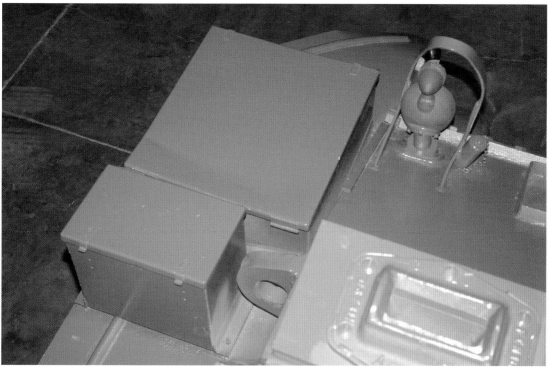

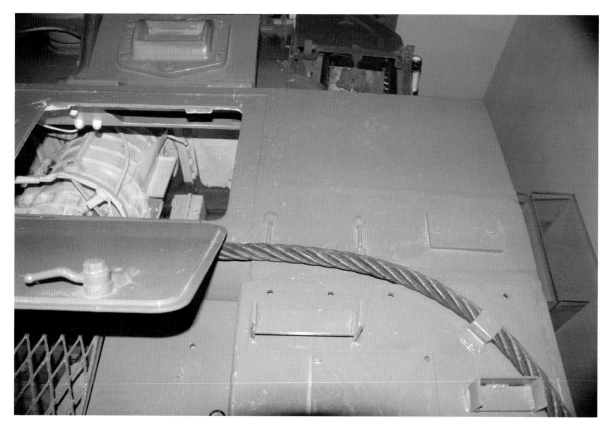

In a view into the right hatch, the transmission is visible, located between the driver's and assistant driver's seat. The transmission used in the M12 was a Synchromesh with five forward gears and one reverse. At the top is the assistant driver's direct-vision door.

Opposite: The two stowage boxes on the front fender are observed from above. Visible on the right bottom of the rear box is a flange by which the box is fastened to the fender. To the right of the rear box and welded to the hull is a lifting eye. A similar lifting eye is on the opposite side of the hull. A rounded rib is present on the fender towards the outboard edge; this was for stiffening the fender.

Above: The right headlight assembly, consisting of a small blackout lamp on top of a service headlight, is observed from overhead. The plug-holder on the inboard side of the brush guard has a plug inserted. To the left of the headlight, two of the flanges of the three-piece final drive housing are visible in profile, with two of the screws and bolts that hold them together. To the far left is the toggle bolt and wing nut that secure the clamp and the cradle of the travel lock.

Opposite above: The travel lock is in the lowered position, viewed from above the assistant driver's hatch. It pivots on two brackets on the frontal plate of the driver's compartment. Below and partially hidden by the cradle and clamp of the travel lock is a ventilator hood.

Opposite below: In a photo of the surviving 155mm Gun Motor Carriage M12 being maneuvered on a transporter, an excellent close-up view is provided of the front end and, in particular, the right sprocket and some of the track connectors. The metal parts of the tracks are painted. (*US Army Field Artillery Museum*)

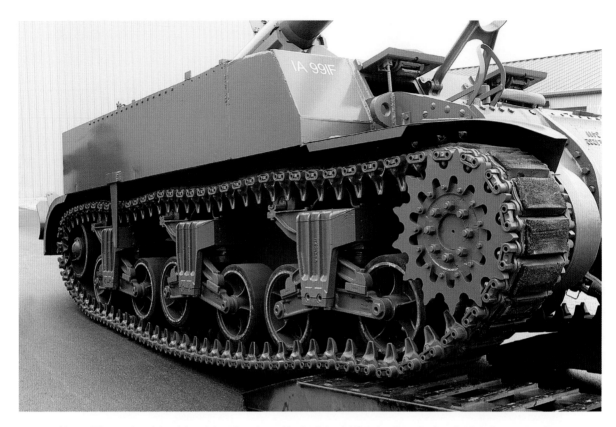

Above: The entire right side of the chassis and hull of the M12 is in view during the loading operation. As the vehicle is partway on the ramps of the transporter, both of the center bogie wheels are suspended in the air. Welded joints of the front of the sponson are in view. (*US Army Field Artillery Museum*)

Opposite above: With the exception of the small shield for the gunner, the crew of the 155mm gun on the M12 had little armor protection. This was largely a result of the original intention to use the M12 primarily in the indirect-fire artillery role, where crewmen were less exposed to enemy fire than in direct-fire missions. The right headlight assembly has been removed. During firing tests of the prototype T6 vehicle, concussion from the gun caused the fixed headlights to shatter, so removable headlights were used on the M12. (*US Army Field Artillery Museum*)

Opposite below: The surviving 155mm Gun Motor Carriage M12 now on display at the US Army Field Artillery Museum, Fort Sill, Oklahoma is a true rarity: the only remaining example of a vehicle of which only 100 were produced. Although the concept of the prototype T6 and the standardized M12 at first met resistance from towed-artillery proponents in the Field Artillery, the M12 time and again measured up to the task, particularly shining as a bunker-buster during the hard-fought Siegfried Line campaign. (*US Army Field Artillery Museum*)

Notes and References

http://lawtonconstitution.net/main.
asp?SectionID=11&SubSectionID=98&ArticleID=31564

This website has some very detailed information concerning certain combat photos (identifying people and places that the official captions do not).

http://www.laxin.net/558thFAB/Photos.asp

T6 and T6 testing (2-3000 series photos)
M12 testing (4000 series)
T14/M30 (4500 series)
M12/M30 field use (5000 series)
M12 Walk Around (7000 series)